DO THEY EVER GROW UP?

101 cartoons about
the terrible twos
and beyond
by Lynn Johnston

MEADOWBROOK PRESS
16648 Meadowbrook Lane
Wayzata, Minnesota 55391

Meadowbrook Press Edition

THIRD PRINTING JANUARY 1980

PRINTED IN THE UNITED STATES OF AMERICA

Library of Congress Catalog Number: 77-82214

ISBN 0-915658-10-0

PREFACE

Now that my kids are five and eight I can't quite believe I survived the terrible twos, threes, and fours. Sometimes my house was a "zoo" and sometimes it was a "war zone". But somehow I survived, wondering all the while why I had been singled out for cruel and unusual punishment.

Lynn Johnston's here to say that what happened in my house happened in her house (and your house) too. We're not alone. We're all in the same leaky, noisy boat together. That doesn't solve the problem, but it certainly puts it into perspective.

I can't think of a "child development" book that will give you as much insight into what really happens during those tender years of tears and tantrums than DO THEY EVER GROW UP? This is Lynn Johnston's funniest book yet.

VICKI LANSKY
author of
FEED ME I'M YOURS
THE TAMING OF THE C.A.N.D.Y. MONSTER

7

8

9

13

14

16

17

20

22

25

27

29

31

33

34

37

40

41

42

43

44

45

46

47

49

50

51

52

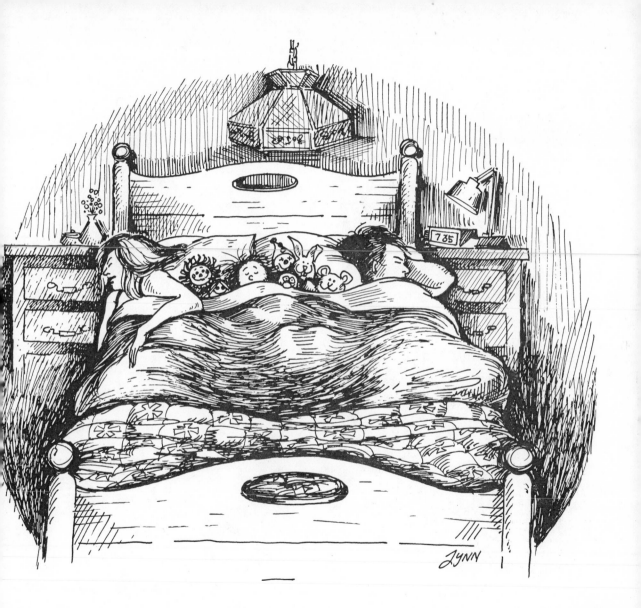

53

54

55

57

58

59

60

63

64

66

67

70

71

73

74

I gotta go to the bathroom...

Lynn

80

81

82

83

84

87

89

91

94

96

97

98

100

101

105

Meet Lynn Johnston

Lynn Johnston is the best-selling female cartoonist in North America with good reason. She draws much of her material from close observation of her family—Aaron (6), Katie (2), and husband Roderick, a "flying dentist" whose practice is based in Lynn Lake (no relation), 800 miles north of Winnipeg, Manitoba. Her deft, humorous depictions of life with kids have provided her with material for three books, published by Meadowbrook Press, and now she has a family comic strip, "For Better or For Worse" running in newspapers throughout North America.

& Her Books:

DAVID WE'RE PREGNANT!!
101 laughing out loud cartoons that accentuate the humorous side of conceiving, expecting and giving birth. A great baby shower gift, it's the perfect way to bolster the spirits of any expectant couple.

$3.45 ppd.

HI MOM! HI DAD!
A side splitting sequel to DAVID WE'RE PREGNANT! 101 cartoons on the first year of childrearing that puts all those late night wakings, early morning wakings, and other traumatic "emergencies" too numerous to list.

$3.45 ppd.

DO THEY EVER GROW UP?
This third in her series of cartoon books is a hilarious survival guide for parents of the tantrum and pacifier set, as well as a side splitting memory book for parents who have lived through it.

$3.45 ppd.

PARENTS' BOOKS 'N BUYS

FEED ME! I'M YOURS
By Vicki Lansky

America's #1 cookbook for new mothers. Tells how to make baby food at home plus delicious, nutritious alternatives to junk food for pre-schoolers. Over 200 childtested recipes. Spiral-bound.

$4.45 postpaid

THE TAMING OF THE C.A.N.D.Y. MONSTER
By Vicki Lansky

#1 New York Times Best-Seller! Tells how to get your children to eat less sugar and salt. Over 200 recipes and ideas for better snacks, desserts, brown bag lunches, traveling meals. Spiral-bound.

$4.45 postpaid

PRACTICAL PARENTING
Newsletter edited by Vicki Lansky

Every issue is packed with problem-solving ideas that have worked for other parents. Plus practical tips that will save you time, tears and money . . . and help you to be a better parent. Easy and fun to read. (6 bi-monthly issues) **$5.00**
(add $1.00 in Canada)

BOOKS Price (Incl. Pstg. & handling)

- ☐ DAVID, WE'RE PREGNANT! Lynn Johnston $3.45
- ☐ HI MOM! HI DAD! Lynn Johnston $3.45
- ☐ DO THEY EVER GROW UP? Lynn Johnston $3.45
- ☐ FEED ME, I'M YOURS Vicki Lansky $4.45
- ☐ THE TAMING OF THE C.A.N.D.Y. MONSTER Vicki Lansky $4.45
- ☐ FREE STUFF FOR KIDS The Free Stuff Editors $3.45

- ☐ WATCH ME GROW 5-yr. record keeping/ calendar album $9.00
- ☐ BEST BABY NAME BOOK Over 10,000 names to choose from $3.45

BUYS

- ☐ BABY FOOD GRINDER Make fresh baby food in seconds. $7.00
- ☐ Practical Parenting Newsletter (6 bi-monthly issues) . . . . $5.00 Add $1.00 in Canada.

TO ORDER BY MAIL

Please send me the books and/or items I have checked above. I am enclosing $_____ in check or money order.

Please allow 4-5 weeks for delivery. (This offer expires Dec. 30, 1982.)

Name _____

Address _____

City _____ State ____ Zip____

MEADOWBROOK PRESS
16648 Meadowbrook Lane
Wayzata, Minnesota 55391